Written by Billy Treacy
Illustrated by Richard Watson

Cora jumped out of bed and wiggled her arms in excitement. Today was her birthday!

'Ooh, I love birthdays!' she said to herself.

It was still early in the morning. Cora decided to go to the shops while her friends were asleep.

She left Netty a note. 'I will be back soon,' she wrote.

Find Netty in the picture. **How many** balloons is she holding?

When Cora had gone, Netty came out from where she'd been hiding.

Then came a knock at the door. It was Ralf and Scooter.

'We saw Cora leave,' said Scooter excitedly.

'Now we can set up for the surprise party!' said Ralf.

Scooter **Ralf**

0 1 2 3 4 5 6 7 8 9 10

Ralf is holding two balloons. Scooter is holding two **more** balloons. **How many** balloons do Ralf and Scooter have **altogether**? Use the number line to help you.

They put everything for the party on the table.

'We've got party hats, a banner, and balloons,' said Scooter, checking his list, 'but what about food?'

'We could all make something before Cora gets back,' suggested Netty.

Good plan! Let's come back with food.

Cora's birthday!

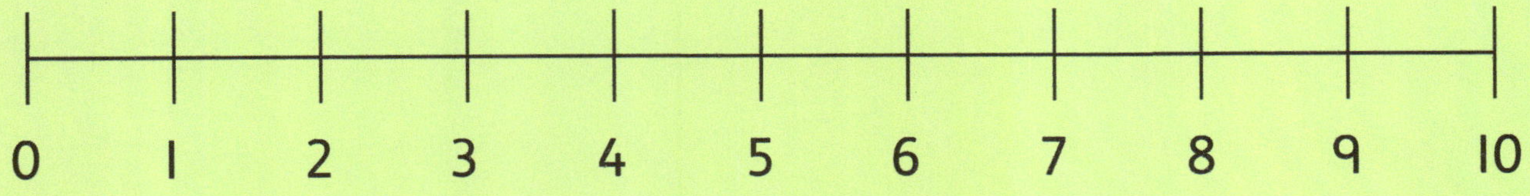

0 1 2 3 4 5 6 7 8 9 10

Netty had two balloons. Then Ralf and Scooter arrived with four **more** balloons. **How many** balloons are there **in total**? Use the number line to help you.

Back home, Ralf stood in his kitchen, wondering what to make.
'I know! I'll make a birthday cake,' he said. 'Cora loves cake.'

Ralf made a big sponge cake. He put some strawberries on the top, then decided to **add** some **more**.

0 1 2 3 4 5 6 7 8 9 10

Ralf had three strawberries on his cake. He **added** two **more** strawberries. **How many** strawberries are there **in total**?

Meanwhile, Scooter stood in his kitchen, wondering what to make. 'I know! I'll make a birthday cake,' he said. 'Cora loves cake.'

Scooter made a big fruit cake. He put some cherries on the top, then decided to **add** some **more**.

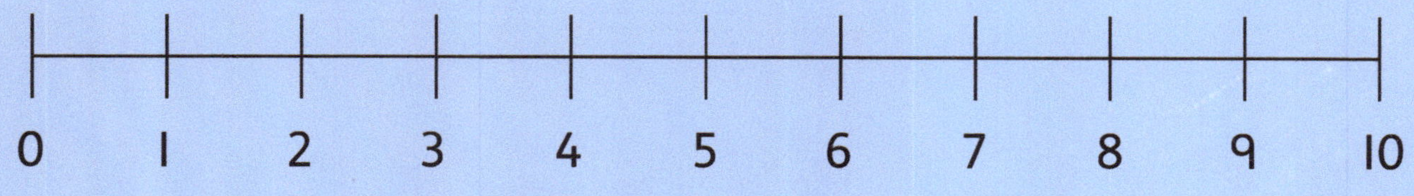

0 1 2 3 4 5 6 7 8 9 10

First, Scooter had five cherries on his cake. Then he **added** some **more** cherries. Now Scooter has eight cherries. **How many** cherries did Scooter **add** to his cake?

In her house, Netty stood in her kitchen, wondering what to make.
'I know! I'll make a birthday cake,' she said. 'Cora loves cake.'

Netty made a big chocolate cake. She put some chocolate buttons on the top, then decided to **add** some **more**.

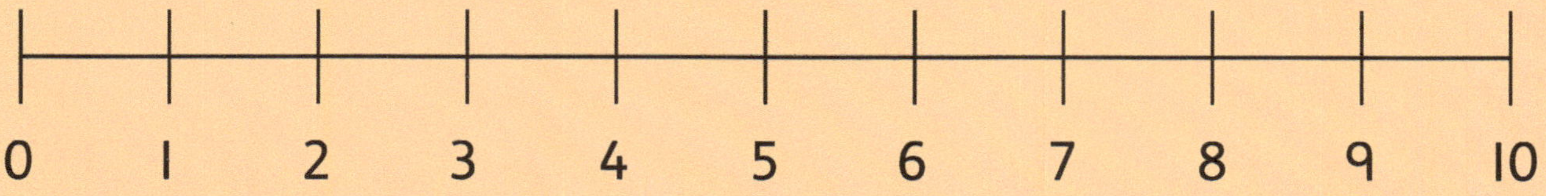

0 1 2 3 4 5 6 7 8 9 10

First, Netty had four chocolate buttons on her cake. Then she **added** some **more** chocolate buttons. Now she has nine chocolate buttons. **How many** chocolate buttons did Netty **add** to her cake?

Ralf and Scooter returned to Netty and Cora's house with their cakes in tins. They all grinned at each other, excited to show off their party food.

However, when they took the lids off their tins, their smiles disappeared. They had all made cakes!

'Cora doesn't need *three* birthday cakes!' said Netty.

'Hang on,' said Ralf. 'I know just what to do.'

'What's that?' asked Scooter.

'If we put the cakes on top of each other, we can make one giant cake,' explained Ralf. 'After all, Cora loves cake!'

'That's a great plan,' said Scooter. 'Let's make it monster!'

How many layers does Ralf's sponge cake have? **How many** layers does Scooter's fruit cake have? **How many** layers does Netty's chocolate cake have?

Netty put her chocolate cake on top of Scooter's fruit cake. Then Ralf put his sponge cake on top of Netty's chocolate cake.

How many layers does the giant cake have altogether?

‘Now we need to put candles on the top,’ said Scooter.

‘We can’t even reach the top!’ replied Netty.

Ralf looked at Scooter. ‘If I lift you up, you will be able to reach,’ he said.

Ralf lifted Scooter up so he could sit on his shoulders.

'Be careful up there!' Netty warned.

Scooter leaned forward so he could put the candles on top of the cake.

0 1 2 3 4 5 6 7 8 9 10

There are five candles on the cake. Scooter is **adding** one **more** candle. **How many** candles are there **altogether**?

Scooter leaned too far forward. He put his hand on the cake to stop himself falling.

The cake swayed from side to side ... then fell over with a giant SPLAT!

Just then, Cora returned from the shops. She looked at her friends covered in cake. She looked at the room covered in cake.

'We're sorry, Cora,' said Ralf. 'We wanted to surprise you with a big birthday cake.'

Cora started to giggle.

She opened her bag and took out a box. Inside was a very nice, very *un*splattered birthday cake.

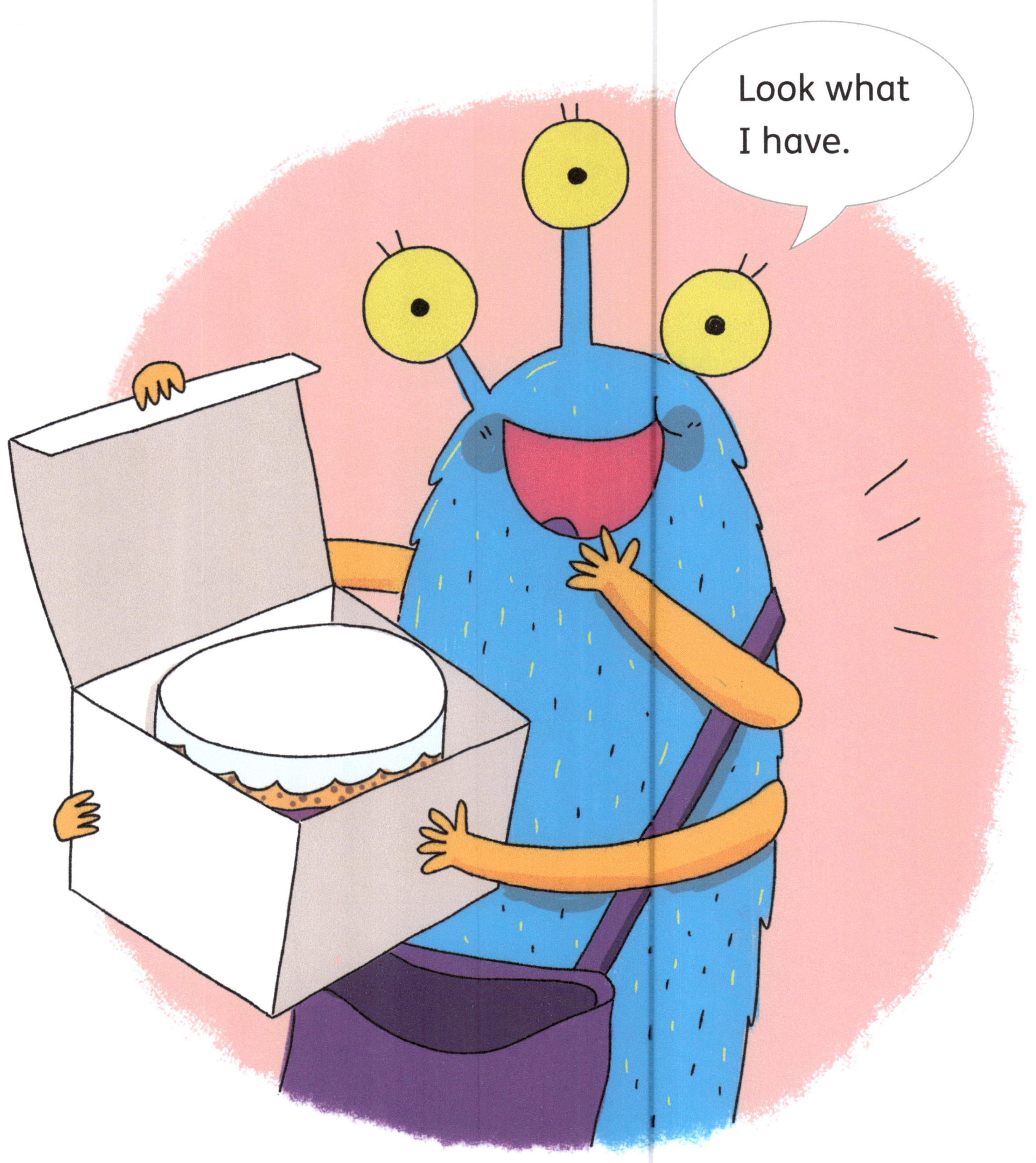

‘Let’s share this birthday cake instead!’ said Cora.

‘Oh, yes please!’ said Netty.

Scooter put the candles on Cora’s cake.

How many candles are on Cora’s birthday cake? **How many** candles is Scooter holding? **How many** candles are there **in total**?

The four friends cleared up and then sat down to enjoy Cora's birthday cake.

'You should make a wish,' said Ralf, before Cora blew out her candles.

Cora didn't need to make a wish. It was already the best birthday ever.

Cora's shopping

1. The number line shows that Cora had some apples in a bowl, then she **added** some **more**.
   How many apples did Cora start with?
   How many apples did Cora **add**?
   How many apples does Cora have now?

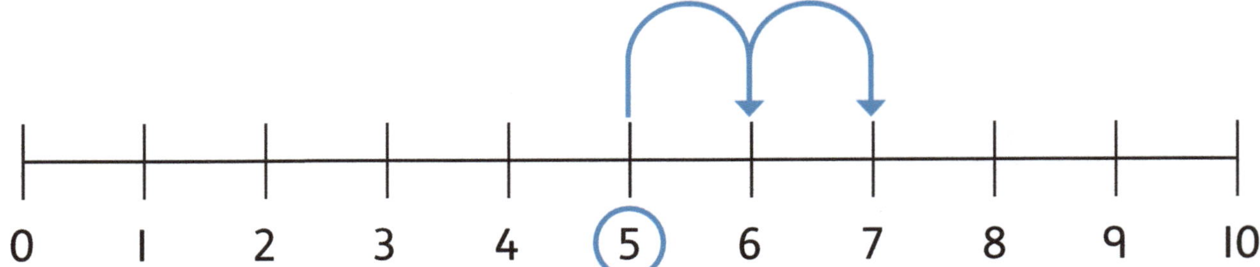

2. The number line shows that Cora had some eggs in a box, then she **added** some **more**.
   How many eggs did Cora start with?
   How many eggs did Cora **add**?
   How many eggs does Cora have now?

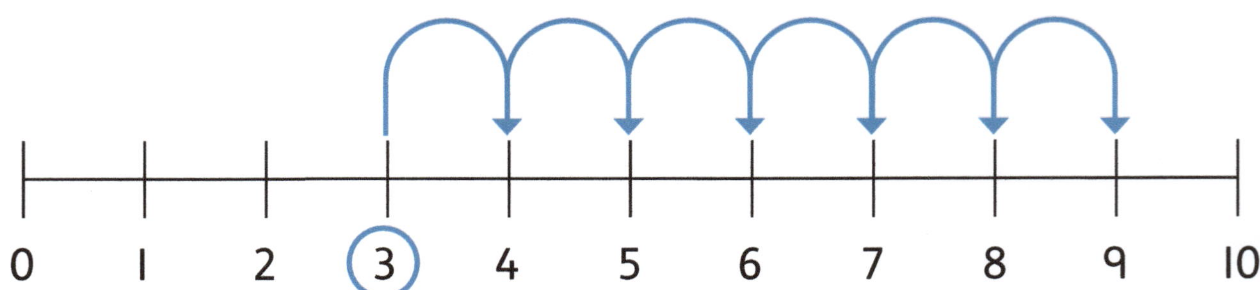